D0997139

SMALL HANDS
BIG IDEAS

© 1988 Tony Hart

Hart, Tony
  Small hands – big ideas.
  1. Handicraft
  I. Title
  745.5′024054   TT160

  ISBN 1–85219–007–8

All enquiries and requests relevant to this title should be sent to the publisher, Bishopsgate Press Ltd., 37 Union Street, London SE1 1SE

Designed by Tony Hart and Gill Harris

Printed and bound by
Singapore National Printers Ltd

SMALL HANDS
BIG IDEAS

TONY HART

BISHOPSGATE PRESS LTD

ACKNOWLEDGEMENTS

So many Children, Parents and Teachers have contributed so much to this book and it is to them that I give my thanks. Without the children this book simply couldn't have happened. Without the teachers it would have been frivolous. Without the parents we wouldn't have had the children! Everyone has given much more than I had any right to expect. It has been a delight to meet them, to work with them and to learn from them. Grateful thanks to:

Mrs Barbara Fox, County Staff Head, Avon.

Mr Davies, the Staff and Children of Abbots Leigh School, Bristol.

Mr Steve Chope, Headmaster; The Staff and Children of Parracombe VC Primary School, N. Devon.

Mr Barclay, Headmaster; Mrs Margaret Wilson, The Staff and Children of West Kilbride Primary School, Ayrshire.

Mrs Marianne Adams, Head of Preparatory Department; The Staff and Children of Ballyclare High School, Co Antrim.

Mrs Anne McVean, Head of Pre-Prep Department; The Staff and Children of 'Chestnut' Department, Hazelwood School, Oxted, Surrey.

Mrs Heather Clarke, Headmistress; The Staff and Children of Longacre School, Shamley Green, Surrey.

Miss Dianne Hollow, Headmistress; Mrs Sandra Hartop, The Staff and Children of Wonersh and Shamley Green C of E First School, Shamley Green, Surrey.

Mrs Madeleine Lamperd and Family.

Mrs Pat Adams, Chairman; Surrey Pre-School Playgroup Association.

Carolyn Williams.

To my friend and Associate Roc Renals for his tremendous help in organising and accompanying me to many of the schools and for his invaluable contribution to the book of photographs of the children.

All photographs by the Author and Roc Renals unless otherwise stated.

p 53 (The Elizabethans)   Wo Hill
p 98 (Paper making)   Jim Farquarson
Cover Photograph   Carolyn Williams

CONTENTS

Alexander 5.

Children and their Art. Here they are shown within the age range of 1 to 7 years. The examples shown include Marbling, Printing and Painting, Drawing and Collage.

INTRODUCTION

The paintings, drawing and modelling done by children should have an appeal to everyone. Not only because we were all children once upon a time but because we can all learn so much from their artwork and take a great deal of pleasure in it too.

In recent years Art has been found to be therapeutic, an aid to dexterity, observation and learning. It promotes a cultural interest, allows the young artist to make a statement and, best of all brings a sense of achievement. After the age of 8 many children become self conscious about their ability to create pictures but in this book you will find no such lack of confidence.

As a one time Art Teacher I taught in a Public School, a Technical College, a Mental Hospital, and a Prison. They probably learned less from me than I did from them but I have never forgotten the benefit we all derived from working together.

Very young children go through the actions of creating long before they even know what a pencil or crayon is. These actions can be pretty destructive but if directed into another channel can bring about something graphic which, eventually, the child realises came from him.

We are lucky to have pre-school playgroups, Nursery Schools and places where very young children are looked after. 'Looking After' also means entertaining, interesting and teaching. Very hard work. From a very early age, under 1 in some cases, I have found that a child can do more in Art than we give them credit. They will readily adapt to a method of producing graphic work that we may consider way outside their abilities. Painting, drawing, modelling and printing are arts open to all children, even the severely handicapped, who derive immense satisfaction from their personal achievement.

I hope this book will encourage some of you to use the ideas, in the book with very young children. I can hear your cry: 'Who's going to get it all ready and who's going to clear it all up?' I know. But try it out. They're going to make a mess anyway! Adapt as and when it's necessary.

The evolution of individuals as artists, be they ever so young, starts at birth. We're all different. We learn about the child from the child. We are charmed by their pictures. They are all here. In the early pages I have included a chronological order of pictures from children under 1 to under 8. Study them and compare the ways of drawing. You can make a fairly good guess as to something of the character of the child by what he draws, how he draws and what he uses. Sorry I kept writing 'He'. We see even more from the girls!

As a parent you watch your child grow from the earliest stages of life through all the changes, good and bad. We are delighted with the success like the first grip of your little finger, the first smile and later, the first word. When your child grips your finger you realise it is a real working little being that is quickly going to develop character. This character shows itself pretty soon. The child has a will of its own. There are going to be family battles and skirmishes of the 'I will, you won't' sort but eventually a reasonable, pint sized human being emerges and does quite sensible things like getting from A to B in a fast crawl, negotiating a step on its backside and, less sensibly, scraping and banging on the floor with anything it can get its hands on. The embryo artist has arrived! Nobody in their right mind gives a one year old a pot of paint and a brush. The end result might be entertaining to anyone who didn't have to clear up the mess but, poor Mum. However, a non toxic crayon, for preference, put into the child's hand will immediately be put into its mouth. This, as you well know, occurs with everything; but soon, as with everything else, it will be scraped, scrubbed and banged on the floor or on the tray of the highchair; So – not a bad plan to have a few sheets of newspaper – or, if you're really interested some cheap liner paper, back of wallpaper or anything else you can get hold of – put it under the assault of the crayon and see what happens.

During the first year of a child's life the 'Artwork' is going to look much like this. A series of lines. Not straight lines but almost mechanical curves. This is because the child grips the crayon as it would a spoon or anything else and articulates from the shoulder rather than from the wrist and elbow. This brings about a fairly repetitive series of curves rather like using pencil and compass to draw part of a circle.

'Hattie' was one year old when these scribbles were done. With remarkable foresight I put her on a large sheet of paper and a drawing board in the garden. She did all the predictable things as well as making earthy footmarks which I have not entirely been able to erase. We haven't come to the art of printing yet. The interesting feature to look for here is the point of return from these scrubbing action drawings. We haven't achieved anything like a circle yet but there is a tight curve here and there which, later on will become a much rounder form.

Small children will draw on the floor or at a table. It was interesting to see how Hattie would cope with an almost vertical easel.

Right:
Marker ink on Computer print out paper

Below:
Marker ink on Cream paper

Hattie is now 19 months old. She's no longer a baby but becoming a little girl. Her grip has strengthened and her scribble more controlled. The curves are more apparent and becoming circular. The examples here were done with markers. She progressed from wax crayons and chalks when she recently started to attend a pre-school playgroup. She gets as much pleasure out of playing with the markers, taking the tops on and off and putting them in rows, as she does in drawing with them.

On the left is a very deliberate piece of drawing. She stood at the easel and you can see where the marker has hesitated before changing angle and going on. The colourful scribble on this page was started at her playgroup when she was drawing with other children. I put it up on the easel hoping she might do some more to it. Obviously it was completed as far as she was concerned. Finally I had to be content with getting a photograph of her putting the top back on the marker. I got the message!

11

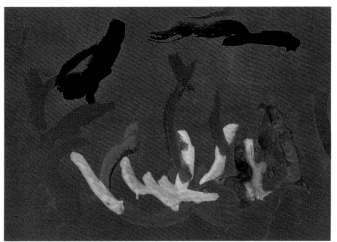

1 YEAR

This would seem an amazing advance from the scribbles of the under 1 year old. It is, of course, an advance but from 1 year on the child starts to use a brush and paint. The action of sloshing paint about and dabbing and dragging the brush over paper brings something new – form and colour. Some of these forms are highly satisfying; either because they look like a nice Abstract or because we see a picture, as we might in cloud formations or in the fire. Happy Accidents. In Hattie's painting (bottom right) I can see a running man and a fish. She didn't mean this to happen. However, after painting the picture (bottom left) she pointed to one of the black smudges and said 'Basil'. Basil is the black cat at the pre school Playgroup she attends.

2 YEARS

Victoria, at 2 years, knows just what she's doing. The drawings may not always be quite recognisable to you, but just look at the orderly way she made line after line of circles. She may decide afterwards what it is that she's drawn, or tell you about it while she's doing it.

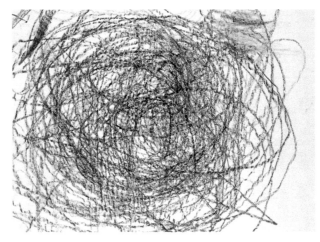

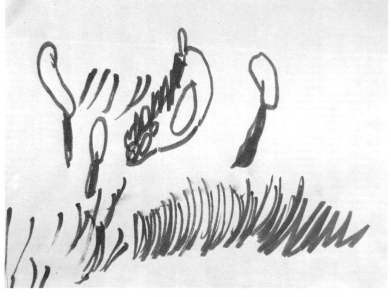

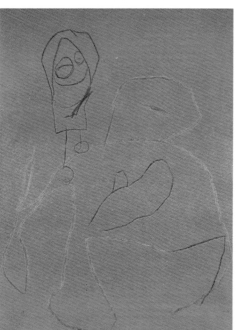

3 YEARS

This self possessed young lady is Clare. At 3 years Clare paints, draws and makes collages. She likes Turtles, Owls and Monsters. You can see perfectly well which is which. The 'Turtle in the Woods' is drawn with trees, thick grass and the turtle, seemingly floating about. Quite natural. Had they been placed in a rather more orthodox way we should have an infant phenomenon which is always somewhat disturbing. Turn the 'Owl Sitting in a Tree' upside down to look at it that way. It is shown as Clare wanted it. I love 'Clare's Monster'. She looks completely in command of the situation, perched up there on his shoulder!

4 YEARS

Louise is 4 years old. She's seen here making exceptionally neat handprints. Her painting, too, is neat. This is a watercolour, 'Rabbit in the Dry Grass'. What a delightful way to use colours. You can see that the brush has been washed between taking up new colours. Nicky, also 4, is at another school. When I came to photograph his picture, done in very thick poster paint, he had, I think, really finished it. He wanted to be painting it for the photograph so applied more thick blue paint to his 'Green Man' which made it rather thinner than it had been!

5 YEARS

By the age of 5 years children's Art is, I think, at its most enchanting. No self conscious work here. The child has so much to interest him that everything that comes into his life is put into his drawings and paintings. Alexander has a liking for mechanical things and has observed tractors and bulldozers and recorded their activities.

Nicola, also 5 years, has made a splendidly splayed hand print from her left hand. Notice she keeps her bandaged finger well out of the way. Her man's head is drawn in crayon. Clare, Louise and Nicola, with a year's difference in their ages, work together. Elsewhere in the book you'll see more of what they can do.

On the opposite page are more drawings and paintings by 5 year olds. Nicola is using a home made 'brush' made from a piece of foam rubber. Bruce has printed a house, using bits of polystyrene. Paul has made a drawing of one. Sonia has painted (and presented me with) a portrait of 'Mr. Tony Hart'!

6 YEARS

These pages show exactly what happens to a child's mind and drawing at the age of 6 years. It's now possible to detect, by results, the creative ability of these young people.

Laura, at 6 years, is putting much more into her excellent crayon drawing of the clown. By cutting it out and displaying it against the dark background it is given a further boost as a picture.

Mark, at the same age, is drawing well. His interests are those of all normal boys of his age. The 'Fairground' picture is a paint print. Card edge or polystyrene pieces have been used to print the lines and forms that go to make up the wheels and girders that give us an almost Impressionist picture of the Fair.

A selection of Mark's pencil drawings that show the interests of a 6 year old boy.

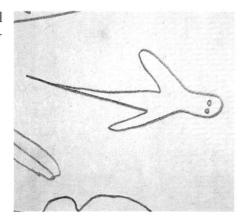

At 6 years, Emma has drawn her dinner. This has been drawn with a wax crayon or piece of candle and the subsequent wax lines have been developed by brushing over with blue ink.

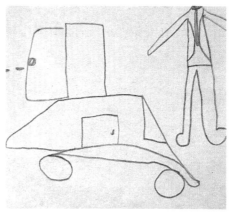

7 YEARS

These are the drawings and paintings of the oldest of our artists – the 7 year olds. At this age techniques as well as a style can be seen. Catherine, at 7 years, is versatile with a sense of design that can be seen by her printing from a polystyrene block and her colourful design of linking circles. The colour is well used again in her clown picture.

Warren's three part picture shows the stages of making a wax transfer monoprint. The 7 years olds have no difficulty in making these pictures. The process is to coat a sheet of paper with a scrawl of differing colours of wax crayon. This is then turned over onto a fresh sheet of paper and a drawing made with pencil or ball point pen. The colours are transferred to the second sheet of paper leaving a negative image, the coloured version and the original drawing.

Harriet's Flower painting has come off particularly well because of her clever use of paint. It is nearly opaque but still allows some outline to be seen which makes the flower forms attractive. By using white for the large flower against the darker background the picture is given the feeling of another dimension.

Katherine has given us a Snow Scene. Drawn and painted in white against a dark blue background. With a stencil used for drawing flasks (Chemistry Class, I expect) she has produced these imaginative characters.

21

RUBBINGS

Rather like printing. Rubbings can be made from practically any flat surface that has a texture. The choice is immense. Such surfaces include engraved objects embossed books, linen and hessian wallpaper, the grain of wood and some floor coverings. Card, paper and natural things like leaves are good too.

In all cases the rubbing must be made with a wax crayon or the sort of hard wax sold for making brass rubbings. The process is simple. Place bank paper, or detail paper over the object which is to be rubbed, hold it in position, if necessary, with masking tape. This will peel off cleanly unlike transparent sticky tape which damages the surface it's stuck on. Rub the paper with black or coloured wax crayon until the pattern of the design is seen clearly on the paper.

Children sometimes make rubbings by accident when drawing with crayons. If the table top has a pronounced wood grain the lines of the drawing often becomes interrupted because of the uneven surface underneath. Once this is understood they have fun by putting things like bits of paper or leaves underneath just to see what happens when rubbed over with wax crayon.

In the following pages I have shown some examples of what might be done with the sort of textured materials that can be found about the home.

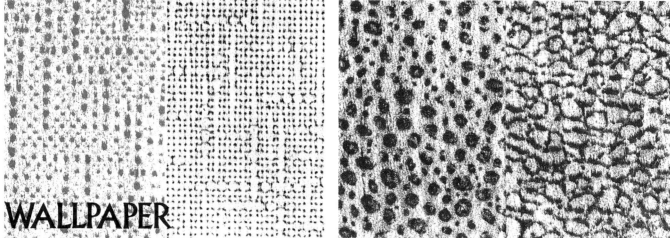

WALLPAPER

Wallpaper, especially the heavy textured sort, makes an excellent material for rubbings. The photograph and other examples show how either side of the paper can be used to obtain different textures. In each case coloured wax crayon was used.

BRASS

Brass rubbing is a popular craft today. Many towns have a Brass Rubbing Centre where anyone can to to make their own rubbings from the glass fibre facsimiles of Church brasses.

Permission may be obtained from Church Authorities to make rubbings from brasses in Cathedrals and Churches, but today it is being discouraged as the Centres give as good results and lots of help.

I found a brass tray with an engraved design that made an excellent rubbing. Use thin detail paper which you can stick to the brass, temporarily, with masking tape at the corners. Use wax crayon or brass rubbing wax.

WOOD GRAIN

I find wood grain gives the most satisfying result for wax rubbing. Look for it on cut planks, floor boards or furniture. Especially old seats and pews in Churches. The rubbing at the top of the page, done with red wax crayon, was from a Church pew.

The blue rubbing was made by using a piece of wax candle on white detail paper. The rubbing could hardly be seen, of course, but after rubbing it over with a piece of ink soaked cotton wool the negative image of the wood grain came to view.

Rubbings like these can be used to good effect as material for a collage. Children can cut their own rubbings into shapes and stick them onto coloured paper.

FLOOR COVERINGS

The textured, vinyl type of floor covering makes a splendid base for a rubbing. Here you can see the sort of floor I mean. Children could work together to cover a large area of paper and then, perhaps, use it as a background for cut-out pictures, a giant chess board or whatever took their fancy.

EMBOSSED BOOKS, ETC.

These are particularly attractive. We all have our favourite books which may have an embossed cover. Children can make a rubbing of "Alice" or "Winnie the Pooh" if you have an embossed edition.

On this page I've shown the result of three wax media. The black is the brass rubbing wax called heelball. The red is ordinary coloured wax crayon and the green is oil pastel which is splendid for transfer prints and drawing, but not so good for rubbings.

My rubbing of Mr. Punch from a bound edition is not made by rubbing white wax crayon over blue paper but by using a candle instead of the crayon. The white paper was then rubbed over with an ink soaked piece of cottonwool. The ink – or you can use water colour – won't stay on the candle wax so a white line image appears.

28

Probably one of the most attractive rubbings is that of leaves. It seems surprising that anything so delicate would not squash under the rubbing, but they are capable of giving results like these. Ferns are good, so are many grasses. Very strong, hard leaves like laurel are not so good. I haven't even tried to make a rubbing from holly!

I thought the rubbing of the leaf here would be more attractive if I coloured the white paper yellow. This I did after I'd made the rubbing. Remember that water colour paints or ink will not stay on the wax. It doesn't matter what colour wax crayon or what colour you paint over it, the two colours will stay the same.

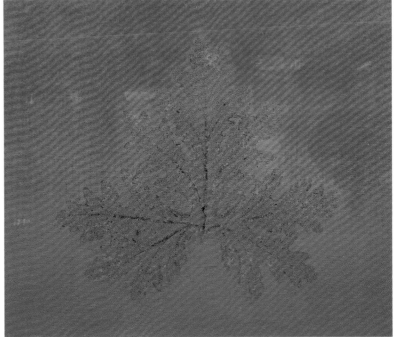

PARRACOMBE SCHOOL

If you know North Devon you probably know Parracombe. A stone village on the Western edge of Exmoor. The Church of St. Petrock must have been visited by many. But when I went to the village it was to the little white walled Parochial VC Primary School to meet the children who were going to do some rubbings and paintings for me. The staff were seemingly as enthusiastic as the 5 to 7 years olds who have provided these pages.

Steve Chope, the Headmaster, turned out to be as kind as had been his letters to me before allowing this visit. On a return visit to the school some weeks later, I arrived to learn that everyone had gone to the swimming baths in Ilfracombe but were expected back at any moment. Sure enough, five minutes later a sound of singing and chatter grew louder as Steve, like the Pied Piper of Hamelin, rounded a bend in the hilly lane followed by the whole school. Country bred children who live and learn in the countryside.

We started to make rubbings, using coloured wax crayon on pieces of paper. The children cut simple shapes – rectangles and triangles – from bits of card and used these as a basis of design. Most of these were abstract while some had an end result in mind, ships or people. They were all intrigued with the effect that paint had on the rubbing. Some really beautiful results came out of this session. In particular was the realisation that realism in Art is neither essential or, indeed, always desirable.

Oliver is 6. His rubbing has been made by placing triangular shapes cut from paper to form a design, then placing paper over these and rubbing with green wax crayon. This he has done three times then washed over with yellow paint.

Tara Jane, who is 5, has used cut out shapes to make her rubbings, but has used two colours to achieve her patterns. After the first rubbing with one colour the paper has been shifted and another colour applied. Different colours in paint have been used overall.

The Blue Tower and the satisfying brown and orange abstract were made by John who is 7. Kim is 6. Her Triangular cut out shapes have been thoughtfully placed and overlapped. This has brought about another satisfying design.

Kim and Caroline, at 6 years, have both used their cut-out card to be seen as rubbings. Using orange paint to heighten the design and, in Caroline's case, to show up the white wax.

David, at 5 years, has rubbed yellow wax crayon over half his picture area then covered it all over with red paint. The paint has dried leaving little red globules on the wax which gives it this pleasing effect.

Vanessa, also 5, has placed some cut-out triangles under the paper. She has used wax crayon to draw lines rather than rub overall. This has brought about another pleasing effect.

Before I left we all went out to the garden that the children are creating. They had started to make a pond, to study pond life, a bog for bog plants, a butterfly garden and a series of trenches in the form of a Celtic Knot. These were to be lined with local stone given them by friends in the area.

That was a few months ago. I have just paid a return visit to see how the stonework was getting on. It was half term but three of the children Toby, Lucy and Claire were there to show me how they had been constructing the walls. They are going to put a Time Capsule in the centre. Next time I visit the school there'll be a mass of flowers in their garden.

A few years ago I contracted shingles. I don't recommend it to anyone. I felt decidedly off colour and had to postpone my usual visit to talk to the children at the Wonersh and Shamley Green C of E First School. A few days later I had sent to me a 'Get Well' book. It was from all my young friends at the school. They had made an impressive collection of their rubbings, mounted them on black paper and made them into a book. Unfortunately the names weren't on them. I went to the school recently to try and identify these four pictures but the children had left. Perhaps someone will recognise these works of art.

'My Cat'

It's my privilege each year to help choose the pictures for the International Mentally Handicapped Art Exhibition, held each year at Mencap in London. There are always hundreds of pictures that work of art. I are particularly interesting to compare the work of, say, a 16 year old, with a mental age of 6, with that of a normal child of 6. Jerry is just such a young man.

'Humpty Dumpty'

This artist is handicapped. She has made this picture by drawing, probably with a ballpoint pen, on thin foil. The foil being first put onto several thicknesses of newspaper. After completion pictures such as these are reversed to become reliefs. They are most effective when displayed in the right lighting conditions. The artist is 16 years old. No, she is by no means mentally handicapped. She is blind.

Nicola 5, Clare 3 and Louise 4

Hattie 1

THE PRE-SCHOOL PLAYGROUP

'Maddie' is one of a number of efficient and caring women who look after very young children when their mothers are away at work. When I went to visit her and the children in her care I found her young guests underneath a large work table playing the sort of game that only very young children can understand. Finding something new to interest them in their visitor they crawled out and our 'Art Session' began.

Handprints were on my agenda so the children obligingly humoured me by allowing their small hands to be inked and pressed to paper, giving the results you see here. Maddie's two daughters and son were there that day to give practical support, help and to organise a running cleaning service before unwanted artwork started to decorate anything other than the paper provided.

The printing ink used was non toxic, washable and waterbased. It was rolled out onto a sheet of polythene. The children pressed hand to ink, then to paper. This was achieved by those aged 1 to 5 with help only when necessary.

I found it surprising that , 2 and 3 year olds could be so careful in making these prints. I wonder if anyone proficient in palmistry could deduce from these early prints anything as to the future for these young people?

Hattie

40

Victoria 2

Hattie 1

Nicola and Clare printing

Louise 4

Continuing our 'Art Session' I introduced the children to a monoprint method that may be new to you. It is a means of using printing ink to transfer a drawing to the reverse side of the paper you're drawing on. Use two sheets of paper and you don't spoil your original drawing as the original and print can be seen side by side instead of having to turn it over to see the print. The children made lots of drawings using the inked up sheet of polythene which, by now, had only a very thin film of ink on it. This method is described in full on page 86 so I won't go into it again. The intriguing thing was that when they turned the paper over to see the printed result they didn't realise that they were looking at a mirror image. Those who could write a bit did eventually see that the letters were wrong but it seemed unimportant to them. It could be as well to let them discover for themselves this interesting phenomenon.

Louise 4

Nicola 5

43

Clare 3

When we went on to painting I wanted to see how the children got on with a somewhat unorthodox brush. I made a simple brush by sticking a small piece of foam rubber (I think it's foam plastic now) onto a stick. It makes a good means of putting paint on paper and you can make it any size or shape you want. The children liked it and found they could cover the paper quickly using the spade shape of their new brush. They also found it made tracks of one width and square shapes.

They experimented with the foam brush, one of cotton wool, which was not so popular, and an ordinary brush.

It's not a bad idea to have a selection of sticks, pencil shape and size, and split one end so you can push material into it, felt, folded pieces of hessian, anything that will soak up a reasonable amount of paint. The foam is really good. A rubber band round the split part will keep the material in place.

Lou 4

Nicola 5, Victoria 3

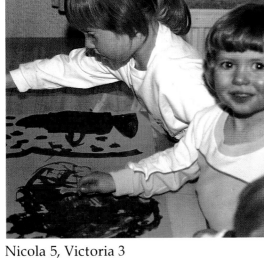

Nicola and Victoria experimenting with brushes

45

Here are some of the children's paintings, the age range is 1 to 5. The children have titled their pictures, either before or after painting them. Hattie, at 1 year, didn't bother!

Victoria's 'worm' was cut out and remounted by me with her approval. Her picture of 'Mummy and Daddy' has, I'm delighted to say, broken the Child Art rule that Mummy is always drawn bigger than anyone! Daddy is on the left!

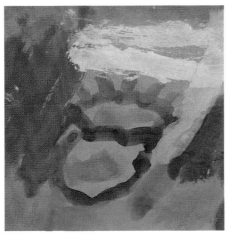

The paintings on this page show much ability for the age of the artists. They are not flukes either. Clare's flowers are remarkable for a 2 year old. Both Lou and Nicola have produced paintings of a higher standard than is average for their years. I remember, years ago, having to produce a 'Rainbow' design for some graphic illustration. I wish that I'd had a 5 year old's manner of interpreting it. So honest – so effective.

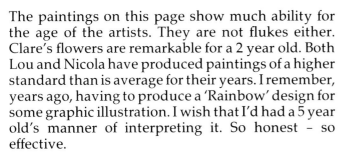

Abbots Leigh School no longer exists. Like a Regiment or The Church a School is a group of human beings. In this case, very young ones. Abbots Leigh was a County Primary School set in a tranquil village in Avon. The County Education Authority regretfully had to close it down and gave due warning so that the few remaining pupils and staff knew what to expect. In the last months of school Mrs. Barbara Fox, County Staff Head, made life pleasant and interesting for everyone while they continued their education. Trips and visits were arranged to places of interest and recorded by the children in various creative ways. I received a letter signed by the whole school – 8 infants and 9 juniors asking me to come to lunch with them. We had a splendid day. They showed me their paintings and drawings and I drew for them. I learnt a lot from them being particularly interested in the artwork of the 4 and 5 year olds. They have contributed some of their work for this book. Here is some of it.

From 4 to 6 years old the children are both enthusiastic and prolific in their drawing and painting. The examples on these pages are by the children of Abbots Leigh School who have been writing as well as drawing. Writing has always been a sort of drawing having developed from pictures into symbols so it's right that the children should record, with the help of their teachers, that which interests them in words as well as in their unaided drawings. At this age it's usual for teachers to write out what the children want to say so that they can copy the letters. No so easy if that which you are copying is isolated from your own paper. This exercise is very good for hand and eye co-ordination as well as for reading and writing. Sophie has illustrated the terrible day on which 'Daddy Dropped her'. The episode has obviously become a family legend bringing everybody closer, especially Sophie and her father.

Do note the interesting 'Y's.

Sophie has drawn another picture in which self interest has waned in favour of the butterflies and silkworms. Attributing human characteristics and features to animals is not merely a childlike way of drawing. Anthropomorphism started in the Ancient World long before Walt Disney!

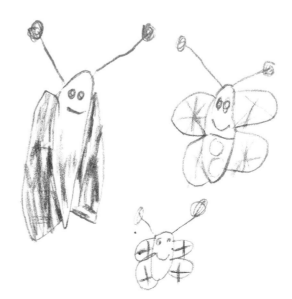

The dentist is looking in my mouth. He is a nice man

Nina is 7 months older than Sophie. She has included her friends in the Ice Lollie picture. A good outward look at life with a nice social comment. The manner of drawing people sitting at table is reminiscent of 16th century manuscripts with their charming disregard for perspective. Nina not only liked the dentist but noticed his patch pockets. The word 'Looking' wouldn't go into the space left in her exercise book so she did exactly what the medieval scribes did! Compare the writing for both these pictures. Copying the teacher's words was easier when they were so close but when they were copied from another sheet of paper it becomes much more difficult. Anyway, I'm sure it was more interesting to draw these personal accounts of life than to write up the diary!

Drawing needs concentration and children always give it, becoming immersed in a creative World that is quite personal. We are, I think, privileged to see the outcome. We notice different ways of drawing at this age. Features, hands and feet. There is always an honest charm.

Here are all of us
Here are all of us
We are making
we are making
blackcurrant ice lollies
blackcurrant ice lollies

This picture of two clowns juggling is quite superb. It's colourful, active and very well observed. It's obvious that Claire enjoyed recording her visit to see the clowns. The whole experience was just waiting to be put on paper as a picture. There is something classic about a pair of funny men, one of whom is tall and thin and one fat. It's all here in the picture. The fat clown, colourfully dressed with enormous boots; a knockabout clown. The other smarter, a classic white faced clown but both together in their juggling act. Note the hands. One clown has the platelike hands while the other has hands that are much more sophisticated with fingers.

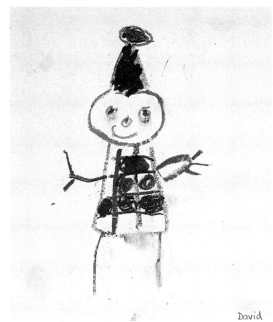

David

All the children had been to see the clowns so here are some more of their pictures. Nina has drawn two, one of them juggling. No hands again on one of them. She often leaves them off. You'll see this again with her Pirate on page 54. David has given his clown some assorted fingers, but Daniel's clown is stretching out his arms to show a full complement of fingers on each hand. It's interesting isn't it? Young artists simply draw just what they feel like.

Style is something that comes later and slowly. As we get older we are influenced by other artists and consciously or subconsciously tend to copy what we like or think clever. Young children, thank goodness, have no such pretensions.

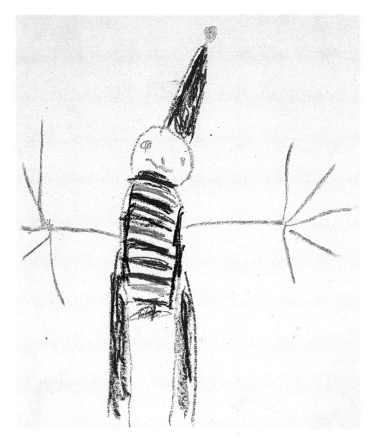

When there was a carnival at Totnes the children went along to see what went on. The costumes fascinated them and became the subjects of drawings and paintings. Andrea called her picture 'The Elizabethan Lady Smiled at me'. What a smile, it outshines the sun which you can also see in the picture as well as the lady's ruff and pearls.

Sophie drew 'The Elizabethan Gentleman with Velvet Knickerbockers'. She took in the quartered effect made by his belt and the vertical stripe on his doublet, she also drew the complicated pattern made up of diamond shapes. Her drawing was cut out and mounted on a dark red background.

The Picture Gallery is important. It's like a Club, an Exhibition and a Diary all rolled into one. It features the interests and artwork of the children. They can look and comment on each others' work. Children being innately honest can make this quite an experience.

The paints of today are non toxic and can be used as poster or water colour paints. Children like to use them either thick or diluted with water and so discover what paint can do for them. Different brushes, with their capacity for giving form with minimal strokes, are an advantage to creative painting. Daniel's painting is called 'A Snow Fight'. To him it was a colourful experience. Bright winter clothing, children rushing about against the white of the snow. It's an Expressionist painting. Daniel wouldn't put it like that but that's what it is – Lovely.

Grandma

This is Sophie's Grandma. Sophie has known her for as long as she can remember. The first thing we notice are Grandma's giant hands. I think that Sophie has always remembered Grandma advancing with wide open arms and stretching them out to her granddaughter. When we are tiny it's often hands that come into, and fill, our field of vision and we remember.

Sophie 5.1

The 'Teddy Bears' Picnic' has been painted in a similar way to Nina's drawing of her friends sitting at the table. They surround the table cloth and can be viewed from any side. In many of the children's pictures you will find the sky painted like this. A blue strip. Later on the child will probably fill in the whole sky area.

Sophie

Nina

The TV Stars Cannon and Ball came to Abbots Leigh. Their appearance and hilarious activities had a great effect and the Gallery benefited.

Nina has expressed her feeling of the visit with a funny character and whirling colour.

Interesting to compare the wide brush strokes here with the delicate pencil lines Nina has used to draw her Happy Pirate.

Nina 5.8

Here is Andrea's picture of the 'Queen smiling at me'. Her Majesty's hat had one of those see through brims so she and Andrea could see each other.

On the left is the Welcome Notice done by the Juniors. I couldn't leave them out. It includes Scott's 'Rabbit'.

Having enjoyed looking at all the pictures, and my lunch, I did some drawing for my young friends before saying goodbye to Abbots Leigh.

Jonathan Moodie, 6 'Hand Tree'

(Courtesy of the BBC)

The pictures on these pages have one thing in common, they both include the artist's hand prints. Jonathan's 'Hand Tree' has been finger painted and hand printed. He's also used cut paper and other collage material. Sophie has used a brush mostly to paint with but has used her hand to make the two prints.

We are mixing painting and printing here. Not mixing the media but the technique – The way of doing it. We can find many ways of applying paint. Rollers, felt, sponges as well as all manner of brushes. The means from which you can make a print are endless. That's what we shall be looking at on the following pages.

printing

All children love to print. There is hardly an object that you can think of that will not make one. Finger and hand prints can be made with paint. Corks, bits of foam rubber, polystyrene, wood, cardboard tubes, bottletops all make good prints using paint as do metal objects like nuts, hinges and washers. Anything with a flat surface can be used. In this section I shall also be showing you a way of offset printing from 3 dimensional objects. Children love this. As a start polystyrene shapes cut from packaging material make suitable blocks. The children will not be cutting these so rectangular blocks should be provided with a paint soaked piece of foam rubber in a tin. They will get the hang of printing in no time. They can be encouraged to pick at the polystyrene to make a different shape to print. This makes for a more personal and so more interesting piece of artwork. Interesting too when they make the discovery that a print is a mirror image of the shape of the block. This usually comes about at the same time that they are learning to read and write. The letters and shapes on this page were printed from cut cardboard rolled up with printing ink. The use of a roller will provide various other ways of printing which are included in the following pages. Printing ink comes in tubes, either oil or water based. Obviously water based printing ink is kinder on hands, aprons and the furniture!

'Everything here will make a print'

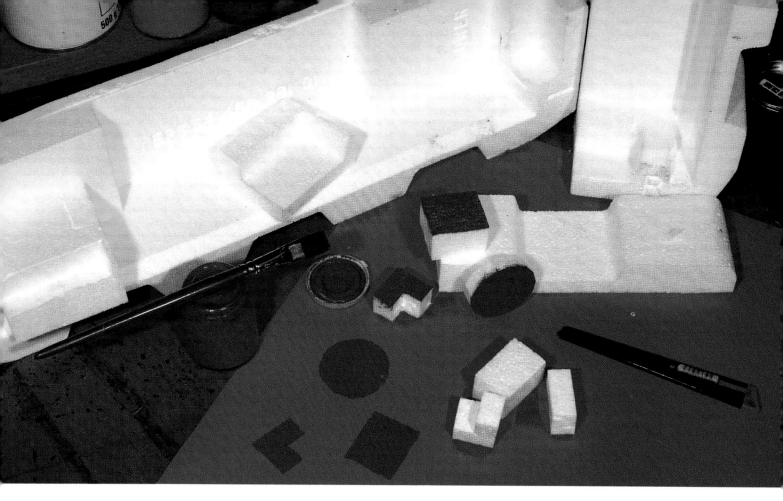

Polystyrene packing material can be cut into block shapes with a craft knife. These can be painted with poster paint and the painted surface pressed to paper to make a print. More or less paint will have different print effects.

 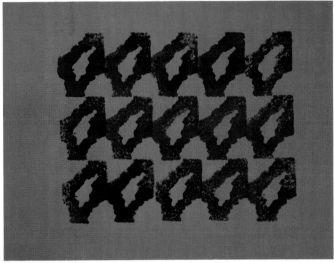

An even better way of applying paint to a block is to dab it onto a paint soaked piece of foam rubber then press it to the paper. Put the painted foam rubber into a tin lid and experiment with the consistency of the paint. Not too thick but not watery. Very young children can pick at one of these blocks to make an interesting shape as they will not be doing any cutting themselves. As time goes by the children will progress from haphazard printing to more regimented repeat prints. There is something satisfying about repeating a shape and even more satisfying when a repeat pattern can be made. Ruled pencil lines will help. They can be erased when the paint is quite dry.

This is using a simple shape like a triangle to make a quite sophisticated pattern. Very young children will not yet have the dexterity to position the polystyrene triangles so as to make the white spaces repeat the triangular shape. Nevertheless they will make random prints. Later on the satisfaction of more geometric patterns and designs will appear.

We saw a picture of some of the never ending list of objects that can be used to make prints. Here are just six of them. A cotton reel, a cork, a marker pen, a steel nut, a cog wheel and an electrical adapter plug. Just one surface of the plug was used to make this print. A tin lid with a circle of foam rubber in it was used to 'ink up' the objects after some black poster paint had been put onto it. Nowadays foam 'rubber' is usually plastic foam and it does the job just as well as real rubber. The cog wheel didn't give quite such a good print as the other objects but this was probably because it had not been properly 'inked' or had not been properly pressed to the paper. No matter, it looks rather nice and certainly has the characteristics of a print.

Cardboard tubes (toilet rolls are fine) make excellent prints. They are easy to handle and children use either a brush to 'ink up' the tube end or use the 'inked up foam' method which is preferable with the youngest. It's interesting to see them using the roll like a brush, dragging it across the paper. This has another result, as you can see. Newspaper has been given a quick once over with emulsion paint, an economic way of providing large sheets for painting.

A 1 year old is capable of printing from simple shapes. Once shown they'll go on for a long time. This sort of 'Artwork' can be made more attractive by finding the most interesting bit and presenting that bit. In this case the page frames it nicely!

'The Balloon Man'

All the prints on these pages were done by 5 and 6 year olds with help! This, under studio conditions and a definite result in mind. Trial prints and suggestions like 'Too much paint, Mark. Try it again!' made it less easy for the children but everyone was pleased with the results. The material used were poster paints, polystyrene shapes and cardboard rolls. We also printed lines from the edges of cardboard strips. The 'bow tie' was printed from an old electrical adapter plug!

Mandy 6, Mark 6 and Ian 5, were the artists.

STENCILS

Stencil pictures is certainly a form of printing inasmuch that you can repeat the design as long as the stencil lasts. Very young children find it a bit much to cope with, mainly because they use the paint either too thick or too thin. Either way the result is going to be a mess. A way of controlling the paint is to use a bit of sponge (foam) and keep just a thin film of paint in a tray.

Children like to make their own stencils. These can be torn from folded paper or cut, if you're in the scissors class. Stencil patterns should be simple. Sometimes the bit you cut out is more interesting than the piece you've cut from. As in the case of the star pattern. Painted newspaper has been used again. Good for painting on and good for cutting stencils.

If young children have made a stencil they want to keep, try spraying it or painting it over with poly-urethene varnish. It will prolong its life enormously.

PAPER PRINTS

Print rollers are very good value. They don't have to be expensive and the children can share a roller to make exciting and rather unusual prints.

The process shown here is printing from bits of cut out paper or thin card. The bits can be as complicated or as simple as you wish. What you will need is – lots of newspaper, water based printing ink, a roller (4 inch is a good size) and some polythene sheeting on which to roll up the ink.

If you simply can't run to a roller try dabbing the ink on to the cut-outs with a foam sponge. The inking of the cut-outs is done on newspaper. Each unit is placed, ink side down, on a sheet of paper and pressed. This can be done with another roller or the back of a spoon, more paper should be placed between the cut-outs and the pressing agent. The cut-outs are removed – finger nails or a piece of thin plastic help this – and the process is repeated.

MONOPRINTS

It means you can only do it once. Very young children find it fun. You need a plastic table top, a smooth piece of plastic or some polythene. The children put poster, or mixed powder paint onto the plastic, mix the colours if they wish but make an overall surface of paint. They can then make patterns while the paint is wet – a little washing up liquid mixed with the paint helps. The patterns or drawings can be done with the fingers, stubbers, made from rolled up newspaper or from pieces of cardboard. When they are ready, a piece of paper, the more absorbent the better (lining or sugar paper) is placed over the work and small hands can press and rub it all over. When removed an impression is transfered. Different thicknesses and consistencies of paint will give different results.

The paint has been applied to a plastic sheet and a pattern made. Paper has been placed over and rubbed. It is being pulled away. Finally it is laid flat to dry.

Another pattern made in the same way.

Hard Brush   Sponge   Roller

The way in which paint, or printing ink, is applied to the plastic sheet determines the textures of the resulting background. Shown here are three ways to apply paint. A scrubbing or nail brush makes a series of parallel lines – the harder the brush the more apparent the lines. Sponge foam gives a very different texture. It can be used to cover the plastic completely or done as you see it here. The third method is to use a roller. In all cases here the drawing has been done with a stylus. A pencil shaped piece of wood with a blunt point.

On this page you see how cardboard can be used to scrap paths in the ink or to make rectangles. The wavy lines were made with a piece of cardboard from which a comb shape was cut.

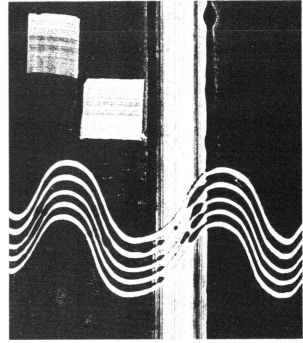

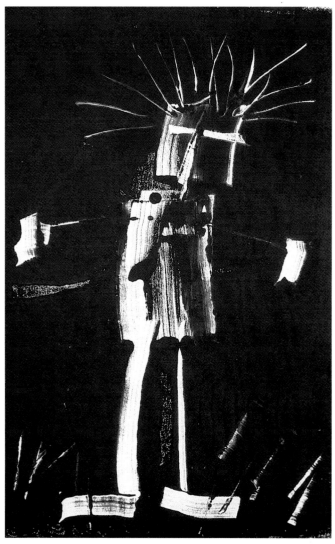

We had some red printing ink on our plastic sheet, it was nearly played out. We decided to see what would happen if black printing ink was rolled over the top. It obliterated the red completely. Adrian made a Robot, drawing with cardboard edges. Bits of the red came to light so a monoprint was made. At least we thought it would be a monoprint. However, the image was still on the plastic so we made another. You can see both results on this page.

The two small pictures show another Robot (or is it a space creature?) because we put even more red ink on the plastic. The second picture is what happened when we put the plastic under the tap to wash the ink off. We thought in the Tate Gallery we ought to get thousands of pounds for it!

More ways of making monoprints. ▶

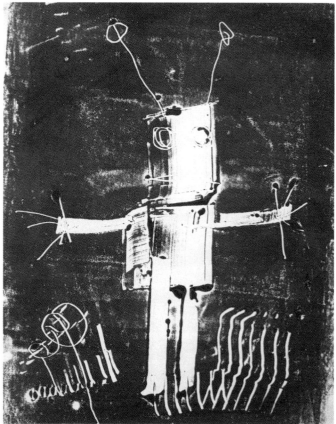

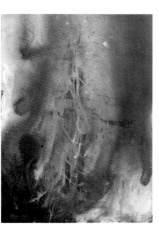

This really explains itself. The rolled up printing ink has had small paper shapes dropped onto it. All we have to do is put paper on top, press, and peel it off. Below is another print done in the same way. You can, after the first print, peel off the paper shapes and make another. The result of that is shown too.

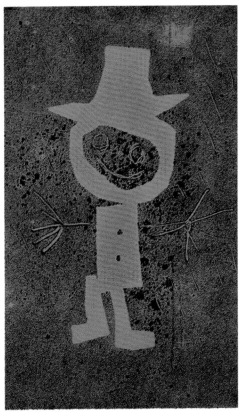

This is a print set up for making one that uses both masking pieces of paper, cut to a special shape, and before printing, adding some drawn detail like hands and face. All these prints give a mirror image result of course, so if any writing goes into the original it must be done in mirror writing.

After these pictures and explanations you don't need to be told how the caterpillar was done.

The roller itself is a good printing instrument. When rolling out a film of ink on glass or plastic you see the mark made by the roller before the whole surface is covered. The picture on the opposite page shows some of these marks. Obviously the marks are determined by the width of the roller. You can make rectangles and squares, straight lines if the roller is just touched to the paper without rolling. If just one end of the roller is touched to the paper a small triangular mark appears, like those triangular wedge-shaped marks of cuneiform writing. If a shape, cut from thin card, is placed under the paper and the roller applied the shape will show up as a print with the area immediately surrounding the print left unmarked. One of the pictures above shows some simple card shapes put together, two overlapping, to form a stylised picture. The other shows what happens when paper is placed over the shapes and the inked up roller applied to it. If you made a frame of the same thickness as the shapes and used that as well, it would be possible to eliminate the extraneous marks. Personally I like these marks I feel it adds character to this sort of print.

This is a more complicated version of the print style we saw before. Here I designed an owl from wallpaper and thin card. Cut out all the pieces required and used them for the final print rolling. It's remarkable what a difference some textured paper can do for a print like this. The wallpaper had a heavily embossed texture that seemed just right for the owl's body. The other bits were of plain card, being smaller they didn't really need to have a texture. If you wanted to give a little texture to plain card all you need to do is to make an indentation in the card with a ballpoint pen or a piece of pointed stick. This will show up well when you come to the ink rolling process.

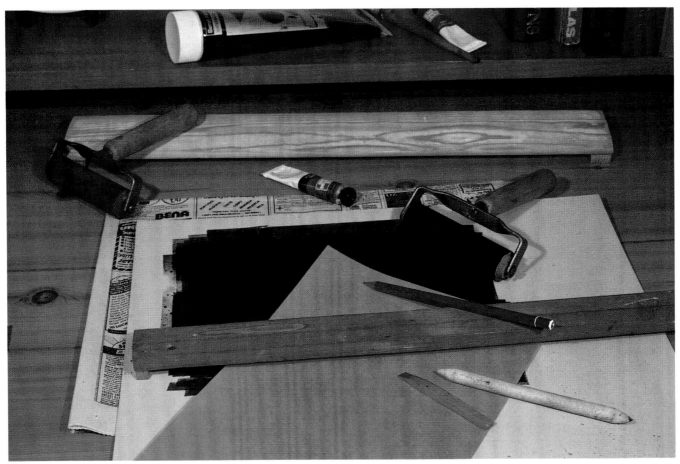

When I was showing you the work of the pre-school playgroup children we saw some delightful monoprints made by using the inked up surface of a polythene sheet over which the children made some pencil drawings. These pictures show you what you need. Instead of a sheet of polythene I've used a sheet of plastic laminate. It was an off cut I bought for a few pence at an ironmongers. It's firmer, of course, and can be washed easily under the tap. The smooth, glasslike surface is very good too. I made a sort of wooden bridge from a strip of softwood. It can be placed across the working surface, clearing the paper by half an inch. Useful for resting the wrist on and stopping any unwanted marks from appearing on the finished print. That, of course, is if you want them stopped!

You'll see from the work shown that the amount of printing ink used determines the sort of line that is going to appear from the original drawing. The fineness of the point used to make the drawing will also have an effect.

Here is an original method of printing for children. It is called 'Offset Printing'. You need some sort of material that can be made to pick up the image from an ink coated object and then transferred to paper. Printing ink or poster paint can be used. I found the best material to be plastic foam pipe lagging. This can be bought in lengths from an ironmongers or DIY shop. This tubelike material can hold a piece of cardboard tube in the middle and be used like a rolling pin. The object from which the offset print is to be made can be inked up by dabbing the ink or paint onto it with a small piece of foam plastic sponge. These objects can be things like scissors, pliers, cog wheels; things that will not usually make a print because the surfaces are rounded or uneven. So the method is to roll the foam sponge over the inked up object. This picks up the shape in ink. Now you roll the foam sponge over a clean sheet of paper. The pictures show these stages and are self explanatory. Try experimenting with other rounded objects, the sort of things you think wouldn't make a print.

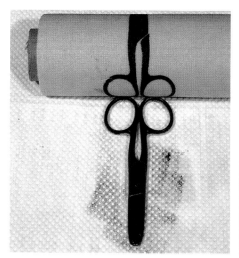

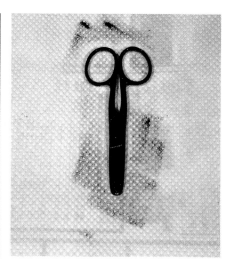

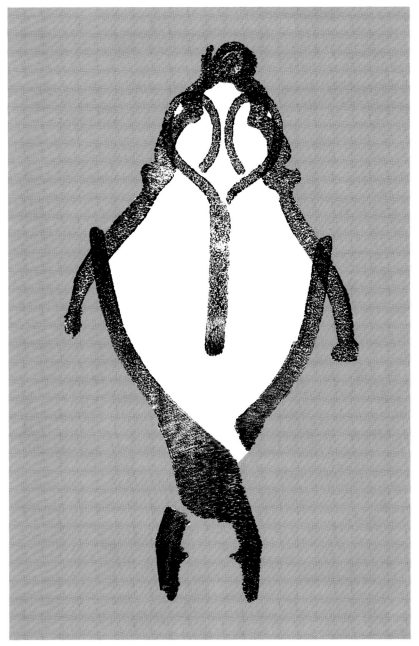

'The Penguin Steps Out'
Offset print from pliers, nutcrackers and scissors. The print was cut out and mounted on a darker background.

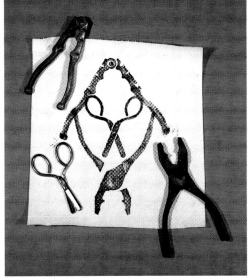

Kitchen paper can be pressed onto an inked object and give a print. Ordinary paper cannot be made to do this without crumpling.

89

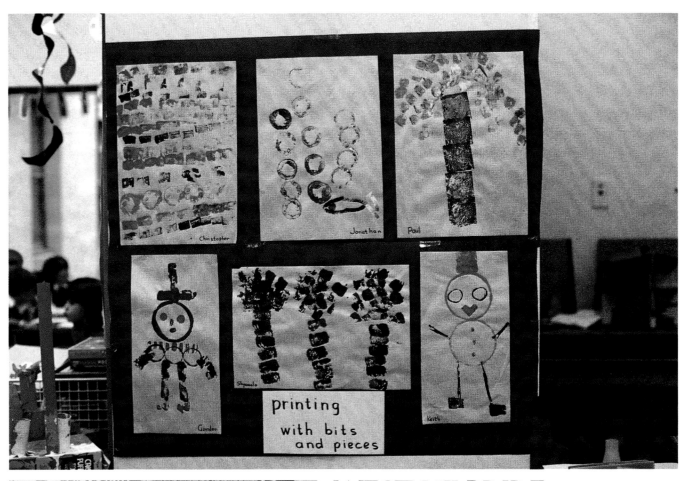

WEST KILBRIDE

At West Kilbride Primary School, in Ayrshire, we were enthusiastically received by the headmaster, Mr. Barclay, who, with his staff, had gone to a great deal of trouble on our behalf to prepare the children for what we hoped to do. This was to see what the children, whose ages ranged from 4 to 7, would do with a selection of small polystyrene shapes if encouraged to print with them. I had sent a supply of these home made shapes along with similar but much larger shapes cut from plastic foam material. These were for the older children. Margaret Wilson, in charge of the younger children, had them beavering away with their little polystyrene blocks which they used in conjuction with thick poster paint. Some simply splendid work came from these youngsters. Here is some of it.

James 4

The younger children printing from polystyrene shapes

91

Some bright colours, a few shapes and your own imagination.

Yellow shows up better on green!

Andrea 4

▲ That looks fun!

◄ And it was. The thick paint shone in the camera lights.

Art can be pretty serious at ▶
times.

It can also be pretty mucky.
These artists must be the
cleanest in the class. ▼

It's fascinating to watch a child who is used to painting with a brush using printing blocks to make a picture. It's different, rather satisfying too. The block is actually doing some of the work for you as long as you know where to put it! Ben has used his shapes to compose a delightful picture with far more character than a mere arrangement of printed shapes.

Ben 4

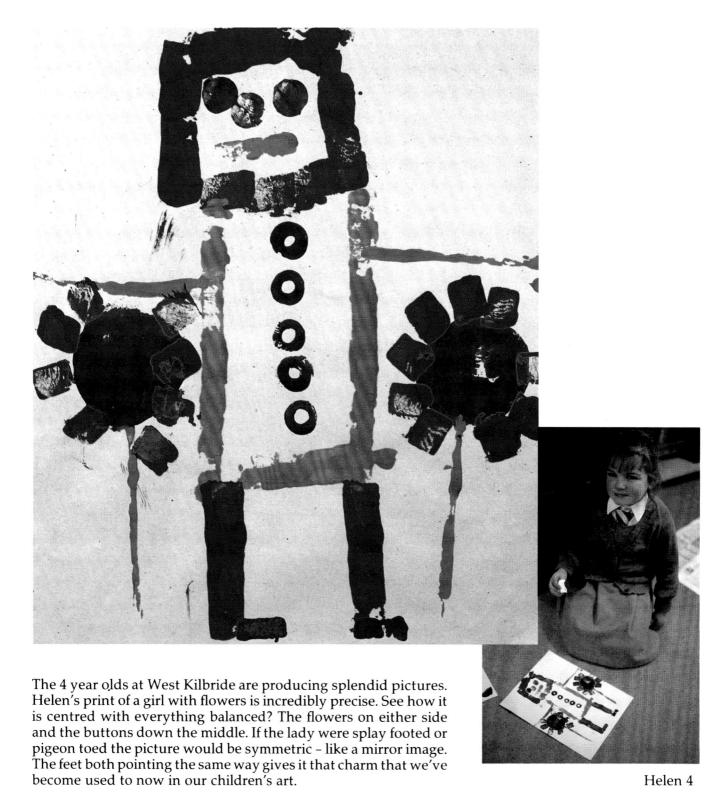

The 4 year olds at West Kilbride are producing splendid pictures. Helen's print of a girl with flowers is incredibly precise. See how it is centred with everything balanced? The flowers on either side and the buttons down the middle. If the lady were splay footed or pigeon toed the picture would be symmetric – like a mirror image. The feet both pointing the same way gives it that charm that we've become used to now in our children's art.

Helen 4

With his 'Tall House', Gavin 5, has used brick shapes to outline the house and left open spaces between the bricks. This 'breathing space' is a useful style in art and often most effective. In this case it adds height to the house.

Effective too are the children's prints when light colours are used against a darker coloured background.

The classroom where everyone works hard.

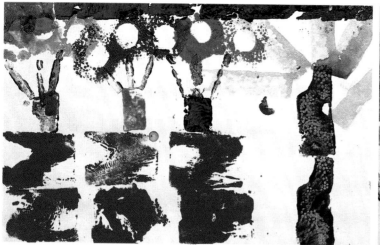

Detail from Becky's print.

The texture of the polystyrene that Becky, who is 6, has used to make her print, has come out in the flower forms to a very good effect. We get a lot of happy accidents in printing. It's part of the satisfaction of the craft.

Two or more thicknesses of newspaper can be stuck together with wallpaper paste then covered with emulsion paint to give a strong and excellent surface for large prints.

Emma and Paul, both 7, are seen making the paper for the older children to print on. They are going to use the larger foam sponge units for making a giant print.

These units of sponge foam have pieces of lightweight insulation board stuck on them to aid holding the units. Latex adhesive is the best for this.

At 6 and 7 years the children were more than enthusiastic to make giant prints. We made up a mixture of black powder paint with washing up liquid and water to give the best consistency for the printing. Plastic trays are useful to hold the 'printing ink' and for dabbing the sponge foam. We also put a very large sheet of polythene under the paper. This was also useful for making trial prints to see if the consistency was right.

SPONGE PRINTING

I think it just as well to give you a run down on what you are going to need for sponge printing. Really it's just sponges, paint and paper to print on. The best sponge I've found is that plastic foam that is used in cushions and mattresses sometimes. It can be found in furnishing shops, department stores and some DIY shops. I found a Handymans Shop nearby where he has lots of off cuts in various thicknesses and sizes. You can buy those square cushion sponges, about 18 inches square. These are rather thick, sometimes 4 inches. You don't really need anything thicker than 1½ or 2 inches. Then a piece of thick insulation board cut to fit the top makes a holding piece and keeps the foam sponge in good shape. I do advise adding a little washing up liquid to the powder paint, if that is what you're going to use, it has four advantages; it keeps the paint from drying out too quickly, it gives a slightly oily consistency which aids the printing process, it makes it much easier to wash the material ready for next time and it smells nice. You'll find a little goes a long way. If a thin film of the 'printing ink' is put into a shallow tray, tin lid or something of that order, and is added to from time to time, the children can 'ink up' from there and a minimum of mess will occur.

Morven, 4

drawing and Painting

Laura, 6

 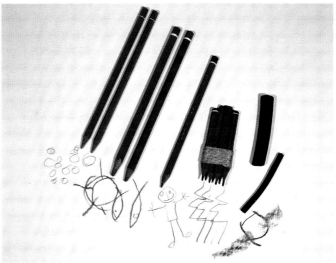

Children today print and draw with a larger range of materials than ever before. Let's look at some of them. Wax crayons and chalks are suitable for all ages. It's the wax crayon that our children all seem to kick off with. It's clean, large and easy to hold. The pencil or pencil shaped crayon comes next. As the child becomes more adept at holding things the pencil is handled in a different way. Fingers and thumb take over from the whole hand grip. Even charcoal might be tried!

Brushes too come to hand during the first year, large brushes used for painting not drawing. I've always seen a subtle difference. Form not line! Unorthodox brushes can be home made so that paint can be applied from plastic foam or cotton wool. Markers of every size, shape and colour flood our markets. What a boon to every artist! More important is that we have permanent markers – indelible, water won't make the colour run, and soluble. Sometimes washable but the colour will run if you wet it. Let's see what can be done.

PRINT AND PAINT

What we are doing is to combine the techniques of both printing with paint and brush painting. In this example a plastic polystyrene food container tray has been cut to a dress shape and used as such. Various jar tops have printed heads and everything else has been painted with a brush, I think. More than likely some finger painting has been used as well. I've found that, in the main, children want either to print or paint, but if left with the choice of one or the other or both, some children will make most original pictures.

Paint sticks, have to me, been a Godsend. You can take a drawing pad, half a dozen paint sticks, one brush and a pen and you are set up for a drawing session wherever you may be. The great advantage is that you have the means of making water colours without paint. You draw and use a brush and water to release the colour from your lines. Of course, you have got to have a little water. In an emergency I've used spit! Very often a child will spoil a drawing done with paint sticks by getting carried away with the exciting effect of brushing with water. But we all ruin our pictures from time to time and learn in the process.

There are both crayons and pencil crayons that can be used with brush and water to pull colour from the original artwork. Aquarelles have been in use for ages. Painting pencils are available in art shops. They are good for delicate work, flower sketches and that sort of thing. Young children tend to prefer the big crayon. It looks like a wax crayon but is soluble in water. Although non-toxic they can give parents a nasty turn when they discover their youngest sucking the red one! These pictures by 4 and 5 year olds were made with the water crayon. Although they haven't the brightness of paint sticks they are a useful means of adding a colour-wash to the artwork.

It's not a terribly good idea to give expensive pastels to young children. 25 pence or more for one colour which is going to get crushed into the carpet seems rather a waste of money and carpet. There are coloured chalks that will fill the bill until the young artist is ready for pastels. They are not, unfortunately, brightly coloured, so the pencil type crayon is probably the best buy. Pastel pencils are also available and will last longer than the high grade pastel.

Nicola, 5, has produced a drawing of the Nativity. Clare, who has an obvious liking for caterpillars, has produced one or more.

Laura, 6, and Ben, 4, brother and sister have both drawn well dressed ladies. Note the eyelashes in both drawings. Alex, 6, has made a remarkable drawing from something I drew on Television to show shadows.

Louise, 4, has made a delightful drawing of a baby animal.

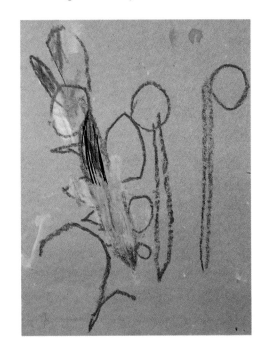

by Alex Konewko Age 6.

111

The drawings on these pages have been done with marker pens. A variety of these can be seen on the photograph above, along with some delightful drawings. We have seen on p. 14, a drawing of a Turtle in the Woods by 3 year old Clare. Here is a masterpiece by the same artist. It is a really brilliant drawing by a 3 year old. She is perfectly happy with a marker as are even younger children. The marker pen has produced a technique in art that simply wasn't seen before the war, 40 plus years ago. When covering large areas with colour, everyone tried to keep a uniform colour or tone overall, using paint so thick it dried to an overall colour, or laying on a watercolour wash keeping the brush moving constantly from side to side so as not to leave tide marks on the paper. With the marker pen this is not possible. The marker ink leaves darker spots at the beginning and end of each stroke. To fill an area with colour means hundreds of short strokes which bring about an appearance, to that area, of a coloured texture to the work that is characteristic of marker pens. I've got used to this in the many pictures I see and rather like it.

Katherine, 7, and Victoria, 2, have made 'a person'. Kathy made a pencil circle and left it to Victoria to put in the features with a red marker.

Ian has used a ball point pen, giving a very fine line, to his drawing. It is, in fact, the original drawing for a wax transfer picture similar to that shown on P.20.

Laura, 6, does such detailed work with marker pens that you can happily frame details from her larger pictures to make one on its own.

TWO SORTS OF MARKER

Earlier I mentioned permanent and non-permanent markers. It is not only possible but very useful to use both on the same picture. Sometimes you want to put a colour-wash on your picture and if the picture has been made with a permanent marker no harm will come to the existing drawing by going over it with water colour. If you tried to do this to a drawing done in non-permanent marker ink what will happen is clearly shown in the picture on the left! In the drawing of the two flowers the outline of one was in permanent ink and the other wasn't. The red brown beast munching yellow grass was drawn in permanent ink. So was the sky. Non-permanent ink was used for the grass and on the body. When a brush and water was used in these areas a rather pleasant colour-wash resulted.

The other characteristic of marker ink, especially permanent markers, is that they 'go through' the paper. Above you can see what happens when you draw on thin paper. The image has penetrated the paper and looks almost as strong in colour as the other side. Some years ago marker pens were given to a class of Eskimo children for the first time. They made drawings on cartridge paper and preferred the image that they found on the reverse side! We experimented with different papers ranging from detail paper to thick cartridge paper to see what happened. You too can see.

Drawing on midweight Cartridge paper using permanent markers.

The reverse of the drawing is fainter.

A few additions to the reverse side.

ADVERTISING·PHOTOGRAPHY·TYPOGRAPHIC DESIGN·ILLUSTRATION

Katherine, 7, continues with her graphic representations of weird characters.

Alex, 4, has used two types of marker to make his drawing of Postman Pat. He is lucky in two respects to be the son of parents who are designers.

Laura, 6, shows her skill again with a detailed picture of a scarecrow in a fabulous field.

116

Rather fun to compare the artistic endeavours of a 1 year old with those of 6 and 7. I wonder if, by seeing the work of two of our young artists several times, you can identify them by their pictures. The umbrella people you have seen before. This is a detail from the picture on p. 104. The frog is by the 7 year old who is always drawing circles.

The linear work of a 6 year old. I'm enchanted with Jamie's drawing. What a difference to the picture when dark areas and a colour, like the door, are brought into the picture.

This is the work of David, 6. It has to be the Garden of Eden, don't you think? And is it God walking in the cool of the evening? Adam and Eve are keeping well out of the way. We must have a close up of them.

WAX RESIST PICTURES

As soon as you realise that oil and water won't mix you understand the working of a resist picture. Wax, like grease and oil, simply will not retain water. 'Water off a duck's back' is true, the feathers are oily. So – if we draw with a wax crayon, then brush or wipe a water-based colour over the drawing the water colour is not retained by the wax which shows up nicely. There are many wax or oil type crayons. The big, ordinary, wax crayon is fine for the job. The light colours, yellow, white, of course, and pale pinks and blues give excellent results, especially when the colour wiped over them is dark. If you can't find white wax crayons you can always use a bit of candle which gives the same effect. Oil pastels have a white among the colours and these are splendid, but more expensive. Water based colour includes any sort of ink except marker ink, which is spirit based. It also includes water colour paint, gouache and poster paint, although it's wise to water the latter down as really thick poster paint wouldn't do the job so well.

   In the section on 'Rubbings' we saw that the texture of what we rubbed, with wax, gave us an image and this was heightened, or developed by the colour put over it. We can use this method to decorate our drawings if we wish. The paper must not be too thick otherwise the detail of the rubbing will not show up. This is shown over the page.

   The means of applying ink or watercolour over the wax drawings are entirely up to you. For large areas cotton wool is best, especially if it is an overall wash of colour. Ordinary blue black ink, which is excellent, does mark the fingers, so the cotton wool can be stuck on a stick to make things easier. Use a brush for small areas.

The character here has been drawn on this paper using a permanent marker. A piece of textured wallpaper was slipped under the drawing and a rubbing made with blue wax crayon on his hat, coat and feet. Magenta ink was used to fill in these areas and the result was as you see.

The same wallpaper was used, but the other side of it, for the ball and the crocodile. The wax crayones were, as you see, red and blue. The yellow ink has made the red look brighter. Used over blue, the yellow ink makes the crocodile appear more green.

"Country Garden"
A collage of wax resist textures.

SCRAPER PICTURES

This is really a sort of homemade scraper board. It has, as a base, wax colour but is covered with paint or ink. Now this is a contradiction to our oil and water won't mix dictum; so you will see that it is going to have to be forced to work! I've found that the best method is to use oil pastels or wax crayon on a sheet of thick paper or card and rub hard, getting it as waxy as possible. We are not drawing now but simply putting down an overall film of wax crayon. Depending on what colour or colours you want to see later, put down a scribble of different colours or put them in lines – whatever you like. Now we have to cover this waxy bit with black ink. If you use Indian Ink and a brush you'll find that a small pool of black just runs about on the waxy surface. By brushing over and over the ink will try to stay but little patches of wax keep appearing. The answer is to make a mix of Indian Ink and black poster paint. This seems to bind the ink and makes it much easier to cover the surface. Don't put much paint with the ink. You can experiment as you go along.

The ink-paint must now dry. When quite dry the scraper card is ready for you to scrape. So it's really a sort of engraving. We use a stylus – a pencil shaped piece of wood – to draw or scrape the picture. The dried black is scratched and scraped to reveal the colours underneath. If you want to scrape larger areas in one go, make a chisel shaped piece of wood and use that.

The pictures opposite show you just what I mean.

BALLYCLARE, NORTHERN IRELAND

It was quite a few years since I'd been in Belfast. The last time I was over it was to entertain the children at an Exhibition in the city. So I looked forward to visiting Ballyclare High School in Co. Antrim. As usual I had corresponded and spoken with the school authorities. We had finalised a programme that would have the 4–7 year olds making 'Resist' pictures, Collages, Paintings and Scraper pictures. I was first met by a boy and a girl from the Preparatory side of the Ballyclare High School. I was reminded again of the charm and courtesy of the Irish. These self-possessed young people took me in to meet Marianne Adams, the Head of the Preparatory Department. From then on it was all go. They showed me wonderful paintings that they had put up on the walls, they brought scraper pictures for me to see, and, straight away, started a new session of 'resist' drawings on the spot. Northern Ireland has problems. It isn't easy for teachers, parents and children, however, the atmosphere here was delightful. The children on top form. So responsive and patently pleased to be helping to add some of their enthusiasm – to say nothing of much splendid artwork – to this book.

Some of the wax resist pictures made by the 4–7 year olds.

Left to Right from the top
Stephen 6, Kate 7, Matthew 5
Philip 5, Susan 6, Darren 6
Emma 6, Gillian 5, Adam 4
Andrew 5, Susan 6, Adam 4
David 4, Lisa 6, Matthew 5

Lisa Carson 5, and Louise 6.

Lisa Burns 6.

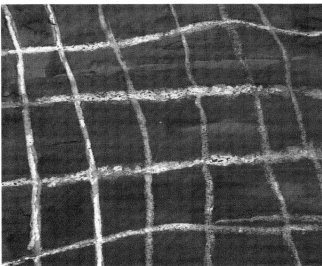

These pages show some examples of wax resist using both white and coloured wax. In fact a piece of candle was used for some of them. Most of the children decided to use blue black ink applied with brushes, but some used watered down poster paint.

On the opposite page are some excellent examples. Christopher 5, is using blue black ink and a bit of sponge to put it on with. He's also done the car, but used another colour.

Gregory 4, made his drawing using red wax crayon. You can see him brushing yellow water colour over it.

On this page, Lisa and Louise, who sit together, have already made pictures of a cat and a dog but are now using red paint over their latest artwork.

Another Lisa has drawn a mesh design and has painted it over with green to produce this tartan effect.

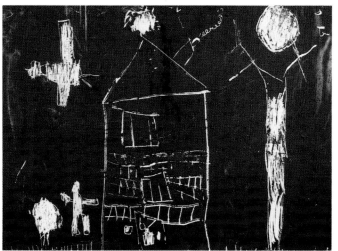

The method of making a homemade scraper board has been fully described on p. 124. These four examples were all done by 7 year olds. I have just been looking again at these pictures. They are all done on pieces of card 9½ × 6½ inches, which gives you an idea of the size. The stylus must have been shaped something like a relief nib as thick and thin scraper lines have been made.

The pictures are by Warren, Kelli, Gregory and Fergus.

It was looking at these scraper drawings with their faint colours from the wax crayon that made me experiment with an alternative method. You might like to give it a try. Instead of coloured wax crayons marking the white card, use permanent marker colours. They dry instantly. Now cover these colours with candle wax. Just rubbing the candle all over the colours which show through brightly. Now carry on with the ink/paint as usual. When dry and scraped you get the effect shown here on the left.

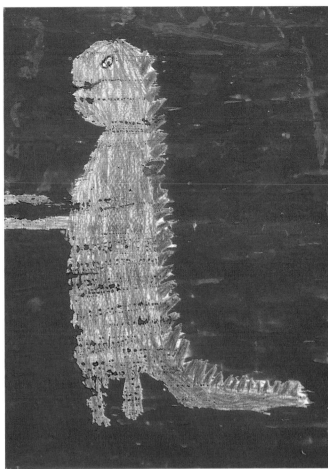

These lovely pictures are a combination of wax crayon drawing and painting. Fergus, Ian and Warren have taken the usual wax resist method a stage further, using more colours over the wax colours and producing fascinating textures where paint has formed isolated globules on the wax and dried. It is so heartening when teachers experiment and adapt known ideas along their lines. So often the results are very exciting.

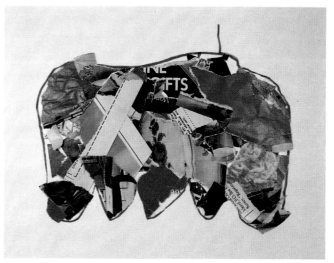

Before crossing to Northern Ireland I had asked Marianne Adams if the children would be interested in making some collages, perhaps using as material, bits cut from magazines. When I arrived they had a rich selection to show. I like to see collages made by young children. It's interesting to see the shapes they use and then where they're put. It's as though you have a second or as many chances as you like, in making the design. Rearrangement of the units is an art of composition. When they're finally stuck down, that's that.

Richard and Christopher are both 5. In the photograph Richard is explaining to me how he drew a lampshade, then used paper pieces to decorate it.

Christopher looks pleased in the photograph and so he should. His collage head is looking pleased as well. See how Chris has manipulated the paper to make the mouth smile?

P.S. I do hope Mary Meredith sees this. Rather a distinction, I feel, to be part of a young artist's collage!

Five more beautiful examples. The aircraft is by Ian 7. Lorna is also 7 and did the 'Artic' lorry. Very well observed – can you see who's driving? Kelli, another 7 year old, made the underwater collage. The fish is so good. Perhaps it's a whale with Mrs. Jonah in residence! Susan 6, did the cat, and Stephen, who is 5, that energetic person striding out to do something – to fight a bull I wouldn't be surprised.

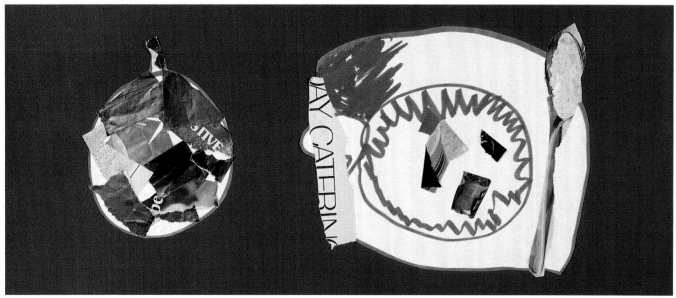

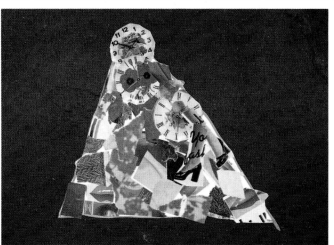

The collage at the top of the page is by Andrew 5 and Gillian, also 5. They have made a picture of their dinner. The apple is Andrew's. Gillian's plate has a knife and fork. Glad to see a green veg. too! Kate 7, the triangular creature with flower eyes and clocks. Roderick 7, has gone to sea with a white cat. Christopher 4, has produced a formidable creature that must surely have escaped from an episode of 'Dr. Who'.

Just to show that a 3 year old is also into collage, here's Clare's cut from metal paper and stuck onto a large white card. After it was done she told us exactly what was there. Here is a key to it:
1. A red person. 2. Aeroplane. 3. Table. 4. Green table. 5. Blue Flower pot. 6. Cradle. 7. Blue Chair. 8. Tennis racket 9. Stocking. 10. Another stocking.

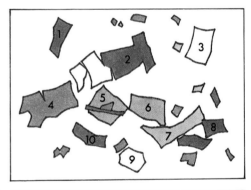

Two delightful masks from Ballyclare

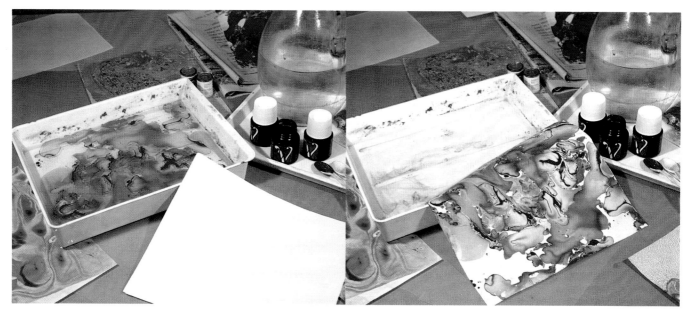

MARBLING PATTERNS

Marbling has been a craft for ages. You see these marbling patterns on old account books and as endpapers. Today it's a fun project that involves dripping oil paint onto water, waiting for a nice pattern to take shape then transferring that pattern to paper. One of those artistic results of a combination of human effort and nature. The human, you, has to find a paint that won't mix with water. Oil paint diluted with turps is fine but very young children don't really need to be bothered with that. The cleaning up poses problems too.

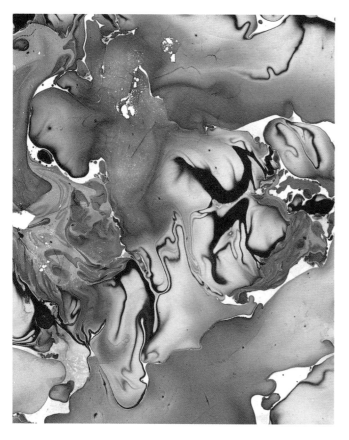

There are paints on the craft market that will do instead. The Pebeo range of craft paints have small pots of glass paint (Coleurs Vitrail) which is very good for marbling as well. If you want something homemade try mixing dry powder colour with a little household oil (I use sunflower seed oil). You have to mix until the powder is absorbed into the oil. The longer you keep it the better.

The process then is to have a tray of clean, cold water and drip a few drops of the oily paint on to it. It will float on the surface, probably in oily globules. Stir them up with a stick or blow to create swirling patterns. When the pattern is good, take a sheet of paper and drop it on the water. Lift off and there is your pattern.

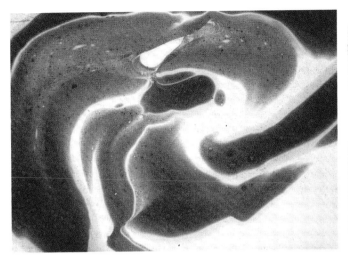

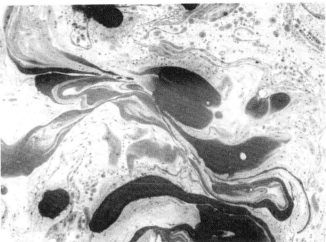

This marbling pattern has a rather different appearance from that shown on the previous page. This one has been made with 'homemade' oil paint. Red powder colour mixed with household oil. The process being exactly as described.

Another pattern produced by the same method. If you use this homemade oil paint recipe, keep it in a jar and either shake it or mix thoroughly every time it's used. The longer you keep it the better it is for these projects.

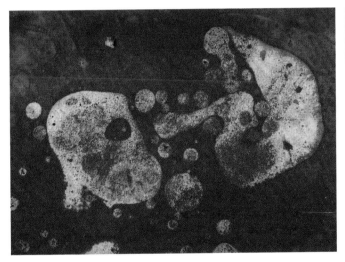

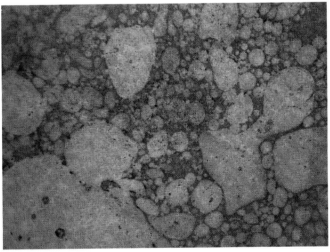

This pattern was made by Nicholas who is 6. The method is rather different. Vegetable oil and water is put into the tray – you must experiment with the amount of oil – then vegetable colouring is dripped in. The effect is different from the preceding patterns but most effective.

The process is exactly the same with the paper lifting off the pattern. The same mixture can be added to and further transfers made.

Nicholas's brother Adam 3, made this one.

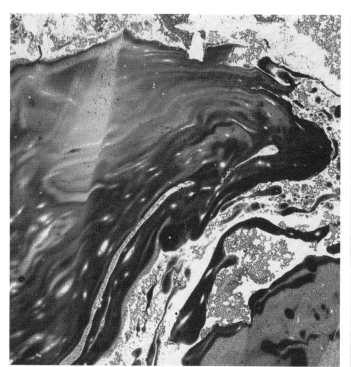

Some of the effects that nature provides when paint refuses to mix with water. These have been made with Red and Blue paint, the patterns being transferred to White, Green and Yellow papers.

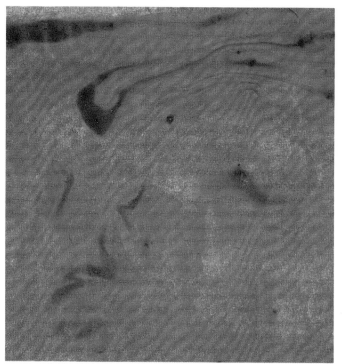
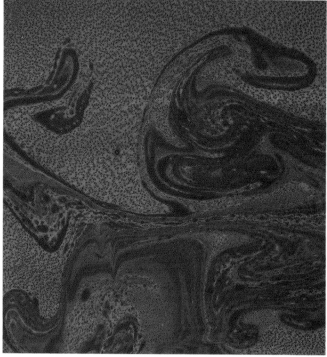

BLOTS, INK AND WATER PROJECTS

At an early age, children making water colour pictures often allow colours to merge without meaning this to happen. The results can be pleasing or mud like. Sometimes the paper gets damp with water sploshing about and even more attractive results occur when colour finds its way to the damp area. Once children realise the possibilities of paint or ink dripped onto damp paper they'll spend hours watching the colour creeping and spreading. What is required is paper, more paper, water, cotton wool, a brush, ink or paint. We can all produce masterpieces like this. The Art is in recognising the good one!

Like Blots, Bubbles have a nice sloshy quality about the making of them. Blowing bubbles that float in the air is one thing, but blowing bubbles and making prints from them is quite another! The way to set about making these prints is to put a little ink, any sort of ink, into a flattish dish. This can be any shape. The shape of the dish will determine the overall shape of the design you make. I've used a small circular dish here. Add a little water to the ink and two or three drops of washing up liquid. Stir this up and, using a plastic drinking straw, blow into the liquid. Bubbles will appear. When they cover the dish you simply lay a sheet of paper or card onto the top of the dish. This bursts the bubbles. When you remove the paper you find a bubble print on it. Just remember to blow gently and for goodness sake don't suck. I know art inks are non toxic today but I still wouldn't recommend sucking. This project is compulsive. It's hard to stop the children making patterns. If you don't get a very good result just blow again to make more bubbles.

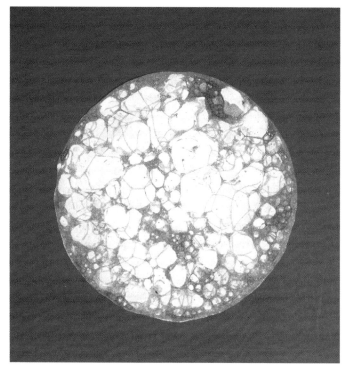

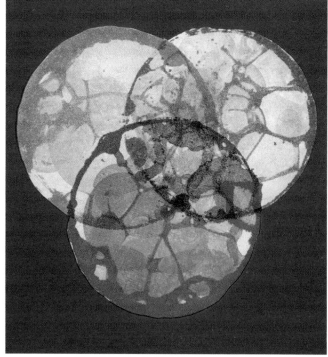

This is a rather attractive way of making a pattern repeat itself one or more times. A sheet of kitchen paper – that really absorbent kind – is folded twice, so the square is a quarter of its original size. Now, very important, fold it not edge to edge but leave single edges so you can get hold of it easily when you unfold it. Now dampen the folded paper, using a brush or cotton wool, but leave dry the two open sides. This makes possible to unfold it later. It's now ready for you to drip or brush on a simple two or more colour design. A brush is probably best as you can dab at the paper and force the colour through. Don't make enormous blobs because the ink spreads on the damp paper. When you're satisfied that the ink has penetrated enough you open up the folded paper. Obviously you take great care. Very small children may want some help at this stage. The result is a symmetrical pattern repeating your original design.

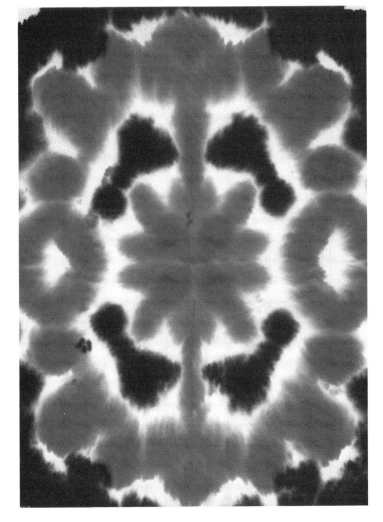

The absorbent quality of blotting paper makes this project possible. Kitchen paper will do but blotting paper is better. You need non-permanent marker pens. Several colours, and use them to make designs or haphazard marks on scraps of blotting paper. These are floated on a shallow tray of clean water and when you're satisfied with the result you take them out and put them aside to dry. Many markers are non-permanent. That is to say the ink in them is soluble in water. As soon as the inked blotting paper touches the water the colour runs producing a soft edge to the design. It's quite fun to make a pattern that follows the shape of the blotting paper piece. This can be either cut or torn. Torn, it produces a ragged edge which is often pleasing. The dry pieces can be used as units for a collage. They look particularly pleasant if stuck to black or a dark coloured background.

A radiating effect can be achieved by making a circular target like pattern and dripping water into the centre. As the dampness spreads from the middle the colours will move outwards to the perimeter.

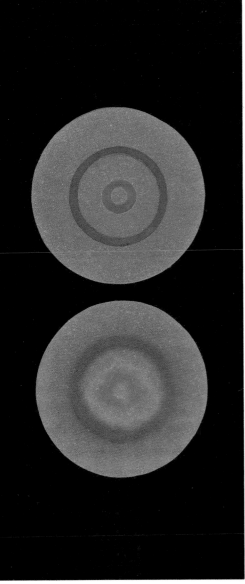

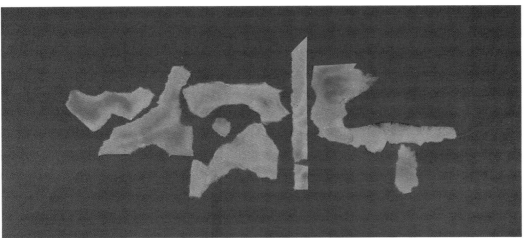

The blotting paper was torn to make the flower shapes and cut for the vase. White and yellow blotting paper was used.

Yellow blotting paper was used for this Abstract. Torn quite haphazardly then arranged to make a design.

143

HAZELWOOD SCHOOL

It was to the younger pupils at Hazelwood School that we went for our marbling and water projects. Anne McVean is Head of the Pre-prep Department at Hazelwood and had been prepared for a sloshy afternoon. She and her kind staff were more than prepared. Three or four class rooms were ready for action. Marbling patterns were displayed and table tops prepared and ready for more to be made.

The 4 year olds had made a special afternoon attendance that day, so we had a full coverage of our hoped for age range, 4 to 7 years. The children had obviously had excellent teaching in Art. Examples of all their projects were displayed throughout 'Chestnut' which houses the pre-prep department. The staff were so helpful and we got a lot done and enjoyed ourselves very much before it was time to pack up and leave that pleasant place on the Kent and Surrey border.

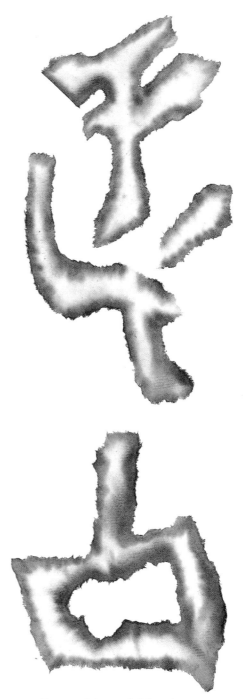

We started off with blotting paper. The older children saw immediately what was required and tore the paper into the shapes they wanted, then marked them with the non-permanent marker pens, which I left with them for future experiments. Everyone crowded round the little tray holding the water while piece after piece of blotting paper was immersed and we all watched to see what would happen. The results were all put to dry and then mounted on black card. The children choosing their own pieces and laying them in position. On the next page you can see what they made.

Some bits of blotting paper were rather like Chinese characters. I tore some more to make the panel above.

Charlie, 6   Philipp, 4
Christina, 4   Jennifer, 5
Stuart, 5   Alastair, 4.

Frances, 6, helps the pattern to develop by stirring things up a bit.

That moment when you wonder if there's anything underneath.

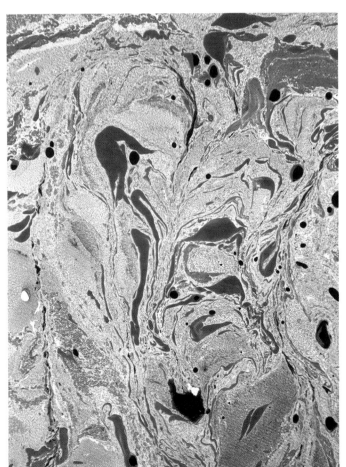

There is, and everyone wants to see what.

The children had already been making marbling patterns but were perfectly happy to go for our cameras.

A pattern by Harriet, 7.

Bayju, 6, making his pattern.

If you mix wallpaper paste with the water to make a thin jelly you can make patterns like this.

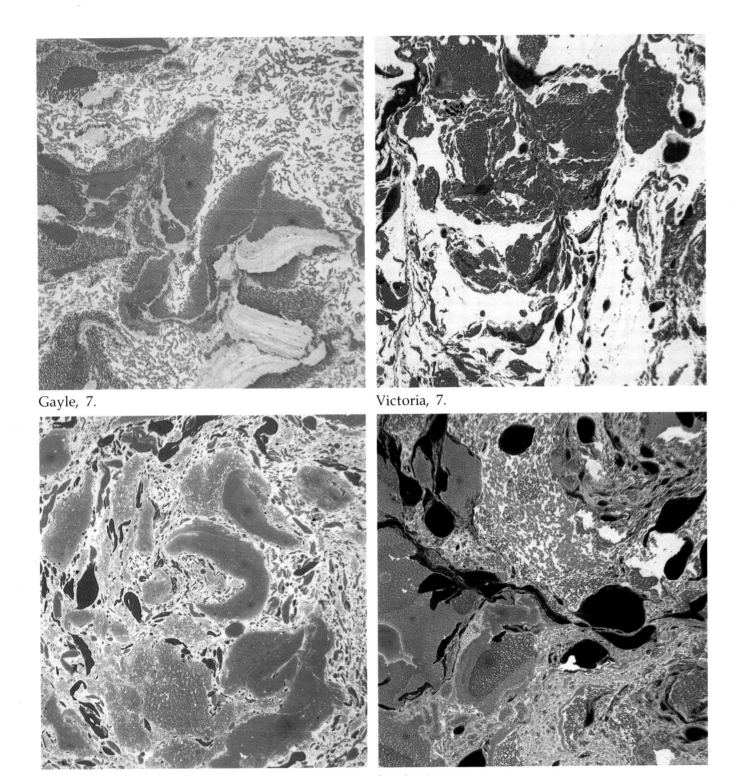

Gayle, 7.

Victoria, 7.

Charlie, 6.

Mark, 6.

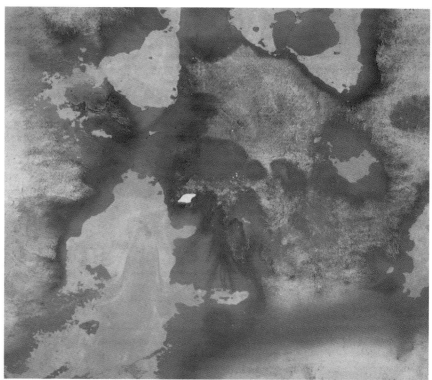
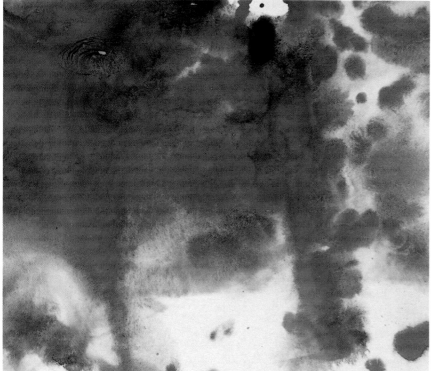

Elizabeth, 7, starts her blot picture, and Jonathan, 5, with his.

Paint or ink on damp paper produces exciting pictures. Henry, 5 on the left, and Anthony, 5, with their blot pictures.

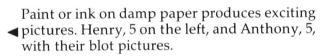

Jonathan's picture displayed.

A completed blot picture.

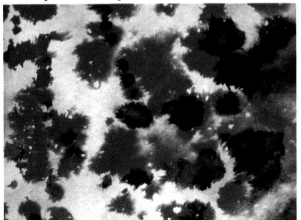

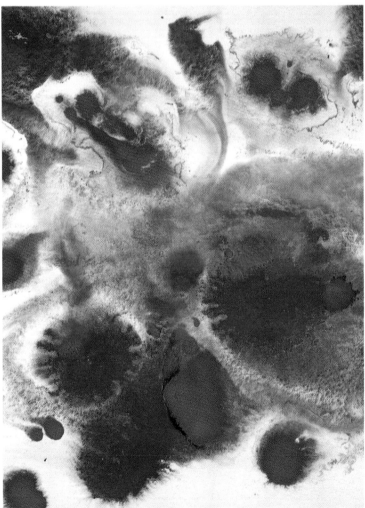

151

Folding the paper on blots produced these symmetric patterns.

I showed the children how, if a design is painted in clean water, ink when dripped on the water will spread. On the opposite page you see how Rebecca, 7, Mark, 6, Jamie, 7, and Thomas, 7, set about making their designs.

Using the method described on P. 141, Martin, 5, and Giles, 5, have produced more symmetrical patterns at Hazelwood.

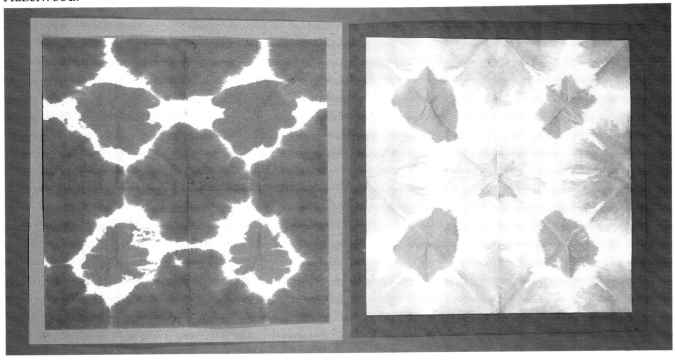

MODELLING AND CLAY PROJECTS

Whether it's sand castles, mud pies, plasticine or clay, all children like to create 3 dimensional things. The first artifacts of man were probably made of clay and we have been using it ever since to make pots, bowls and, in our early years, wiggly worms and sub human creations. Today there are a variety of claylike substances to use. Plasticine and equivalent modelling clay remains always maleable, while other substances, plastic based, can be gently heated to produce an unbreakable hard plastic. Shown here are some amusing models by Oliver, 6, and David, 5, from Parracombe. And from Katie, 7, and the children from Shamley Green.

The children of Wonersh and Shamley Green First School have decorated pages before in this book. They were asked if they'd like to make some sort of relief design in clay – what they did was entirely up to them. They rolled out clay to make a rectangular base and either added units of design or made impressions in the clay. Everyone did something different but on a similar base, so we ended up with a whole series of plaques. On this page we see the work of Melissa, Grant and Lynsey who are all 7.

I was reminded of heraldry – coats of arms, something very personal, when I saw all these attractive plaques. You'll notice that as well as rolls, rods and circles, Mandy has used hexagons in her work. At first sight I thought Jamie's was a spiral, which would have been easier, but he has made a series of six decreasing circles and added a nice economy of impress work to it. Mandy and Jamie are also 7.

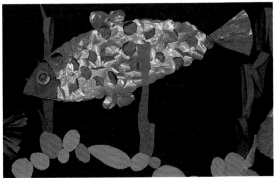

LONGACRE SCHOOL

Involvement by Children with Teachers can be best seen by parents and friends when creative results are shown to all. Work shown at end of term, Art Exhibitions, Plays and Concerts do this. Plays need costumes and scenery as well as performers. A school should allow Children and Staff to have a say in what is going to happen and work together to advantage. At Longacre the children made pictures of the animals concerned in Saint Saens 'Carnival of the Animals', for this was to be performed at their concert. When I saw the designs and costumes I asked Heather Clarke, Headmistress of Longacre, if I might take some photographs for the book. Everyone seemed enthusiastic about this and were splendidly cooperative. So here are some of the 'Animals' in their effective costumes.

David and William. Both 6 years.

When delightful paintings of animals and collages have been made at school it really is a splendid idea to adapt these pictures to become costumes. Apart from the obvious materials most of the headgear was made from card. On these pages you can see how well this has worked out. Here we see Lions, Baby Elephants and Wild Asses. I think Katie, in the elephant headpiece, is a gem! Didn't you love the Fossils on the previous page?

(Back row) Alastair and Lewis
◄(Front row) Nicholas, Dominic and Katie. All from the Nursery Class.

►Katie.   ▼Meechal, Daniel and James. All 7 years.

Charlotte (6), Lucy B (7), Victoria (6) and Lucy W (6) wearing their costumes inspired by one of the delightful pictures made in the school and displayed in a classroom.

The elephant costumes were cleverly adapted from the pictures made by the children. I managed to catch three of the older elephants, between rain showers, in the garden.
Joanna, Natasha and Anna. 7 years.

It's a delight to see the very young children getting together with those a bit older to produce, with help and encouragement from their teachers, something so creative, entertaining and worthwhile.

Annabelle 5, Mark 6 and Alex 5, kindly posed, in their classroom beside a mural of chickens, wearing their own chicken headgear.

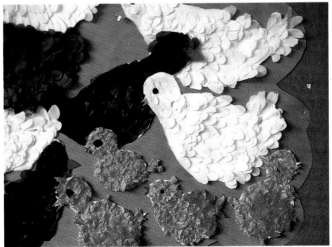

Deedsgrove Playgroup. Ages 3–3½

The pictures on these two pages were made by pre-school and First School children. They were entered for an Art Festival Competition in High Wycombe and won prizes. I always feel that the prizes are won as much by the teachers as by the children. At this age it would be unreasonable to suppose that little or no help had been given. Look at the ages involved. In my experience, as a judge of Children's Art, no teacher has ever tried to tell me that they 'Did it with no help from me'. I wouldn't expect it and doubt if I'd believe it.

Deedsgrove Playgroup. Ages 3–3½

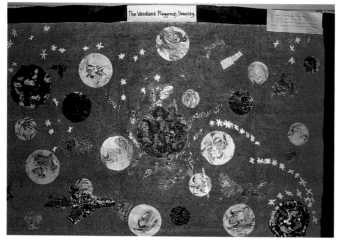

Woodland Playgroup. Ages 3 to 4

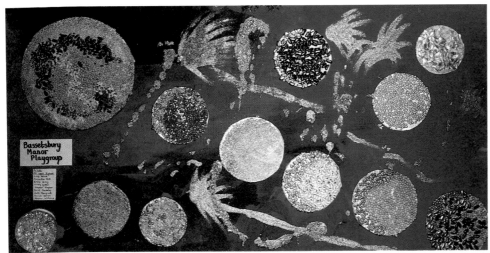

'Half the world is empty
With plenty of room to spare.
The other half is crowded
With people everywhere.

Bassetsbury Manor Playgroup. Ages 3

These pictures have had help in the most sensible way possible. Let the children do as much as is in their capability – make the drawings, cut them out – position them, find the collage bits, do some sticking – and we'll show them a better background, suggest a move here or there and generally make it look even better so that everyone is pleased.

Little Marlow C of E First School.

Chiltern Gate School. Ages 5 to 7

BEACH ART

We've all made sand castles, sand pies and dug moats. We've decorated them with pebbles, seaweed and anything that comes to hand. It's worth looking for beach debris to create even more eye catching artwork. Not all beaches have smooth sand. We can make good use of pebbles, waterworn glass, seaweed and driftwood. Pebbles are found in fascinating colours and in many shapes and sizes. Effective but transient sculpture can be made by balancing pebbles one on top of another. Philip, aged 7, was very good at this on the beach at Lynmouth. Driftwood and seaweed can usually be found high and dry on the beach after high tide.

Using a giant rake, weighted with rock and tied to the back of a motorbike, I made this sinister character in the sand. Mercifully it was removed by the next tide but not before I panted to the top of Brean Down and took this picture. They don't have to be this big nor do you need a motorbike! The octopus is tiny in comparison. A stick will make marks in the sand that can be seen for a long way. Try making marks in the sand like fences so that you can fill in these areas with pebbles, seaweed, driftwood and shingle. A lot of burnt wood can be found too, this gives a good contrast to lighter coloured wood.

Waterworn glass gives translucent colours when wet but is rather dull when dry.

The sort of surface that children work on is important. Sometimes they work at a table, which has to be cleared after every session, and sometimes on the floor. Horizontal surfaces. It's pretty rare for very young children to have easels so that their painting or drawing surface can be angled.

Recently I met up with three children: Yvette, 2, Clare, 3, and Kelly also 3. They were being given the opportunity of trying out a special piece of furniture designed for children to work on. Like a desk it has room for seating two young people, but this piece of equipment has an adjustable top, a plastic covering with pockets for materials and can be angled, like an easel or reversed to make another table top with a cushioned surface suitable for making rubbings, collages and prints. The other side being suitable for drawing and painting. The surfaces can be drawn on or painted as they are washable.

The three young artists soon became involved with a collage, using plastic shapes which stuck naturally to the surface, having adjusted it to the most suitable angle for their purpose.

The author with Clare, Yvette and Kelly.

Kelly and Clare with their artwork.

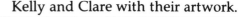